# THE SUCCESS FLOW

## Excelling to the Highest Place

Dr. Geren Gatling

Copyright © 2017 by Dr. Geren Gatling

The Success Flow
Excelling to the Highest Place
by Dr. Geren Gatling

Printed in the United States of America.
Edited by Xulon Press.

ISBN 9781498492492

All rights reserved solely by the author. The author guarantees all contents are original and do not infringe upon the legal rights of any other person or work. No part of this book may be reproduced in any form without the permission of the author. The views expressed in this book are not necessarily those of the publisher.

Unless otherwise indicated, Scripture quotations taken from the King James Version (KJV) – public domain

Scripture quotations taken from the New International Version (NIV). Copyright © 1973, 1978, 1984, 2011 by Biblica, Inc.™. Used by permission. All rights reserved.

www.xulonpress.com

# Table of Contents

About Geren Gatling...................................................... vii
Introduction ................................................................ ix
Preface (Hellhole) ........................................................ xi
Chapter One: Why ...................................................... 13
Chapter Two: True Prosperity/ Prayer Of Salvation ........ 23
Chapter Three: The Success Flow.................................. 29
Chapter Four: Prerequisites-Process-Principles ............. 43
Chapter Five: Counseling-Command-Connection ........ 64
Conclusion: Let The Rivers Flow.................................. 89

# About Geren Gatling

Geren Gatling was a troubled youth whose life was shattered by a life sin. While highly addicted to drugs, he would spend his life in and out of jails and prisons. On October 17, 2010, he was homeless, friendless, and seemingly hopeless. It was on that day that he came into contact with the Savior Jesus Christ after hearing the preached Word of God. After that miraculous encounter, he joined the church and began applying the Word of God to his life. Year by year, he became stronger and the chains that once held him lost their grip. He now has a heart for other lost souls and has a desire to bring others into the saving knowledge of Jesus Christ. He began ministering the Word on World Power Gospel Radio (WPGR), with his new program, "The Kingdom Seekers" radio broadcast. He received an award from the President of WPGR for the top producing program effectively reaching over five million people for Christ. He then founded "The Kingdom Seekers" television broadcast, which airs weekly on The Now Television Network (NOW). Recently, he has formed The Geren Gatling Evangelistic Association (GGEA)

and his whole purpose in life is to advance the Kingdom of God by teaching, preaching, and ministering a healing message to a lost world. His passion for the lost has compelled him to dedicate his life to getting the gospel of Jesus Christ on every available medium.

# Introduction

In June 2013, the Word of the Lord came to me saying, "Your job is to save souls." I already preached on the radio. I put my messages on Twitter, Facebook, and YouTube, but the more I ministered, the more the desire to win souls for Christ increased. As my wife and I stepped out the house one morning, I blurted out "I'm going to write a book." I even told her the book title. The purpose of this book is simple: "God is not willing that any should perish, but that all should come to repentance" (2 Peter 3:9b). I certainly take no pride in my past; in fact, I am embarrassed by it. However, I am willing to put it on display if it means someone would come to know Jesus Christ.

It may be that you are the reason that this book was written. Maybe you know someone whose life is spiraling out of control. Perhaps, like I was, you are an inmate with nothing but time on your hands who stumbled on this book. You may have been given this book by a concerned relative or friend. Whatever the reason, you are either the person in need or the vehicle God is going to use to get this book into the hands of the person who needs it, so please do not take this moment lightly. It does not matter what your current position is, it does not change God's plan for your life. Faith in God can change your current condition. Faith in God can take you from death to life; from the park bench to the pulpit; from crack to Christ; from sickness to health; from poverty to wealth; or, like me, from the hell hole to the radio. To God be the glory!

# Preface

*Hellhole: a place lacking in comfort, cleanliness, or order; an oppressive or unbearable place.*

On October 17, 2010, I stood in Washington, DC on the corner of Galveston Street SE, at approximately eight o'clock on a Sunday morning. The sky was overcast and my mood was sullen. I stood at a city bus stop wondering what in the world was I going to do. I was in serious trouble. I felt like I could not cry out to God; at least not the way that I lived my life. The doctor I knew said according to his knowledge of mental health, I needed to be on medication, which I immediately rejected. I remember his reply: "Do you think these things you are doing are normal?" I knew he was right, but I tried not to hear that. I was sick and weak in my body. I hardly ate anything, and even if I did eat, it was never balanced. I was homeless; I had no ID card, no birth certificate, no social security card, no money, no clothes, no friends, nothing.

My family was tired of me; I was a crack head. This time, my addiction had taken me farther than I wanted to go. It cost me everything. I stood there, knowing in one month I would be standing in front of a judge to face twenty-seven criminal charges. I have never felt so scared and helpless. I could not call anyone; I had burned all my bridges. I felt like dying, but I was too scared to kill myself. I wanted to run, but I had nowhere to go. I wanted to cry, but had cried out all my tears. My mind raced and tried to find a new scheme. Usually, when I was in a mess, I could plot and come up with some kind of plan to get to the next high, the next meal, the next place to sleep, the next person to rob, the next lie to tell, the next person to manipulate, the next victim—there was always one more. Not this day; I had run out of options.

Maybe what people said about me was true.

"You're either going to jail or hell."

"You'll always be a crack head."

"You're a loser."

"You ain't working on nothing!"

"You're just like your father; he wasn't worth a dime, and neither are you."

"Your teacher said every time you show up to school it's like a bad toothache."

"You do know you could have been aborted? They have this needle now that I could have taken one shot and you wouldn't be here."

It felt like everything people said about me had come to pass. How did I get in this hellhole?

# Why? Behavior Reflects an Attitude

You don't need to be a psychologist to know the things that are happening on the outside are a reflection of what is going on inside. From what was I running? For what was I looking? What was I chasing? What have I become? Who created this monster? Why was I running from the law again? Why was I homeless again? Why was I on my way to prison again? Why, why, why, why? *Why*? W-what, H-happened, in my Y-Youth?

I was able to trace some of my problems back to my childhood. Seeds were sown early in my life that had finally come to fruition. If my life were a tree, it would bear several kinds of bad fruit all at once. Each fruit could be traced back to the roots of my childhood. The three major things that I liked to do, and destroyed me, were getting high, having sex, and stealing. The first time I got high, I was twelve years old. I started drinking beer at ten years old. My twin brother and I stole some beer off the back of a truck; it was the same kind of beer we saw in our home and that is how we knew what to take. It was Colt 45™. After that day, I would sneak drinks from around the house when my mom had parties. Then I would take puffs of cigarettes until I was introduced to marijuana.

I was also in a youth gang called The Young Assassinators. In order to be a member, you had to have a family member who was also in The Assassinators, and I did. We would vandalize the neighborhood, steal, fight, and cause chaos everywhere we went. One day, while we were in South Brooklyn, New York at the clubhouse on Fourth Avenue, we put together some Molotov cocktail bombs for an upcoming gang fight. One of the guys on our crew lit up a marijuana joint and he asked if I wanted some. I said yes because in our neighborhood, you were judged by your courage to do something, or if you "punked" out.

When I smoked the joint, I had never felt like that before in my life, and I thought I was in a cartoon and floating. From that day forward, getting high was my passion. Drinking, smoking cigarettes, and smoking weed became my sole purpose for living. Although I was bright in school, it became boring to me. I played hooky all the time with my brothers and my friends. My drug use escalated, and I would soon become the black sheep of the family. I got suspended from school regularly for all kinds of stuff. I once was caught putting thumbtacks in all the kids' chairs in my class. I would fight, disrespect teachers, steal, and cause all kinds of mischief. The whole neighborhood knew I was a problem child.

One day, my brother Vincent took a stick and twisted it in a neighbor's gate. It damaged the man's gate and he was furious. The man told my mom what happened and my mother blew up with anger. There were eight children in our family—six boys and two girls—so we gave our mom constant headaches. My mom has heart trouble and would always complain we were stressing her out. Several times, an ambulance was called to our house for her bad heart trouble.

One particular time, she called the BCW (Bureau of Child Welfare) and they told her to take the worst child out of the house—and that so happened to be me. This time when I was innocent, but I had to pay. The bureau showed up at the house and took me away. I can still remember that day like it was yesterday. It was without question the most traumatic experience in my life and the turning point. I remember crying loudly and looking back toward our home and not understanding why, thinking I did not do anything. Here I was, a twelve-year-old boy being separated from my family. I was devastated and scared. They took to me to a place called Saint Vincent's Home for Boys. I was a stranger in a strange land; things did not get better. In fact, I had gotten worse. There must have been a hundred or more boys in that place. Their ages ranged from my age to eighteen years old. It was a well-structured place in that there was something to do all the time—schooling, counseling, trips, events, sports, and food.

They served us meals that I never knew existed. In my home, we barely had enough to eat, and most of the time we had watered-down grits for dinner, with franks and beans or "wish sandwiches". A wish sandwich is when you have two slices of bread and you wish you had some meat to put between them. In my home, we ate mayonnaise sandwiches, ketchup sandwiches, syrup sandwiches, or butter sandwiches, but this was not the case at St. Vincent's.

They had grilled ham and cheese sandwiches. We drank chocolate milk, orange juice, and sodas. Somehow, all the food and games helped me to mask my pain.

I became friends with a couple of the other troubled boys. We formed an alliance, which bonded us together like family, but it also multiplied our problems. We would get high together, steal, and vandalize the community. When we had free time, we found a "vic," which is short for a victim, and we hunted them like prey. They were easy to find; typically they were people who were careless, nonchalant, oblivious to their surroundings, and usually had a look on their face like they felt they were better than anyone else. We robbed them, snatched their purses and their gold chains, broke in their cars, and broke into their businesses.

We did the same thing with the school up the street from St. Vincent's. We broke into the principal's office and found money and a bottle of gin. We drank the gin as we vandalized the place. We poured paint all over, wrecked the kitchen, and took the spoil. We decided to take the meat slicer and sell it in the morning. As we walked up the street, a police car turned the corner, the cops got out of their car, and they arrested us and brought us to the precinct. While we were there, they searched the neighborhood and found the school was vandalized. When they returned, one of the officers lifted my leg and referred to the design on the soles of my sneakers, which had left an imprint in the paint we splashed around the school. We were *busted!* He kicked me in the chin and called me a word that I do not want to repeat.

The other two boys were older than me, so they took them someplace different. I was twelve years old, so I was taken to the notorious juvenile center Spofford in the Bronx. It was dark when the police vehicle pulled up to the barbed-wired facility. It was a microcosm of an adult detention center. The staff was mean and violent. They smacked us around and cursed at us regularly. The only time I had any peace was when I was in my cell. I was released within ten days and I was so glad to be out of that place. Later, as I walked out of the courtroom with my mother, she said, "I'm taking you home; I thought that boys' home would make you better, but you are getting worse."

That is when I asked her why she took me out of the house in the first place, when she knew I did not damage the man's fence, because it was damaged by my brother Vinnie. My mother said BCW told her "to take out the worst child." So, the damage was already done; the seeds were sown, and the foundations of a criminal lifestyle were laid. I would grow up to become a menace to society, a terror to my community, a pain to my teachers, and a problem to my mother. My issues got me kicked out of school, kicked out of the Army, kicked out of my mom's house, and rejected by others. I had become an outcast.

I have been to several different jails and prisons. I've been through several drug programs. I've seen several mental health counselors. I've been assigned several probation officers and nobody was able to figure me out. Why would a grown man sleep in an abandoned building? Why did I spend every waking moment looking for the next hit of crack cocaine? Why was I promiscuous? Why did I enjoy stealing? Why was I so deviant? Why was I in and out of jail? Why, why, why, why, why?

My mother once told me, "Geren, I went through your old school records and they are all As and Bs. I don't understand why you do the things you do." It felt like everyone always asked me, "Why?" What they did not know was when I took my last hit of crack for the night and sat in some dark place, settling in for a place to sleep, feeling depressed and hopeless, I would ask myself that same question. They did not know when the cell door closed at night and the correctional officer yelled, "Lockdown," I lay in a cold cell crying and asking myself, *why?* I knew I was better than that; I knew I was bright, I knew drugs would kill me, but I liked getting high. Many times, as I walked the streets and saw couples holding hands, going out to eat, and enjoying their families, I immediately felt depressed and asked myself, *why can't I do that? Why can't I have a drink with dinner and friends and go home? Why do I spend all my money on drugs and nightwalkers? Why, why, why, why, why?*

Trips to the jailhouse did not appear to be working. Trips to programs did not appear to be working. Tears and family advice did not appear to be working. Threats from judges and parole officers did not appear to be working. My life spiraled out of control, and I was headed to hell in a bucket.

As I stood there on that October Sunday, on the corner of Galveston Street, I felt hopeless. Spiritually, I knew I was separated from God. Mentally, I was out of whack (otherwise known as bipolar disorder). Physically, I was sick in my body. Financially,

I was broke. I had no ID card, no birth certificate, no debit or credit card, no job, and no money. I was not only broke, but I was broken. As I stood by the city bus stop at eight o'clock that morning, suddenly I heard a voice say to me: "Someone is coming to give you a ride."

Without thinking, I blurted out, "That is the stupidest thing I ever heard; no one is going to give a black man a ride at eight o'clock in the morning in Southeast DC!" Southeast DC is one of the poorest and most crime-ridden sections of the city. As soon as those words came out of my mouth, a white vehicle turned the corner. As I stood in amazement, the voice spoke again, almost sarcastically: "There's your ride."

As I looked closer, I saw the vehicle driver was a woman. So, I spoke back to the voice and said, "Now if that were a man, maybe he would give me a ride, but there's no way a woman is giving a black man a ride at eight o'clock in the morning in Southeast DC." No soon as those words came out of my mouth, the woman rolled down her window and asked me: "Do you want a ride?"

I stood in wonder and amazement. This could not possibly be happening, but it was. The psychologist said I was off and needed to be on medication. Maybe he was right; I heard voices and talked back to them now. Wait a minute—the car was in front of me; this was real. I finally answered the woman, "Yes, I do."

I got into the car and she asked, "Where are you going?"

I replied, "I don't know."

She was a chunky black woman, and she looked at me as if I was an idiot. She said, "What do you mean, you 'don't know'?"

With a shrug of my shoulders, I repeated, "I don't know."

I then proceeded to tell her a part of my story, and explained why I was at the bus stop. The woman immediately drove a few blocks and went up a little hill to the backside of a church. The car stopped in front of the building at 700 Southern Avenue. The church is called Temple of Praise. It was a strange place; the folks there were happy. The men at the front door smiled and shook my hand. Every step I took, people greeted me and smiled; I immediately became suspicious. I thought for sure these people wanted something from me. In fact, two years later, I still did not trust them. It took some time for me to get over all of the suspicion and emotional junk I picked up over the years of being in the streets, crack houses, jail houses, whore houses, and the criminal environment.

I found a place to sit in the middle of the sanctuary. Before I could sit down, an announcement was made asking for all the first-time visitors to stand up, so I remained standing. All the first-time visitors were welcomed to the church by one of ministers on the pulpit. The minister ended his welcome by saying, "Temple, show your love." Out of nowhere, people swarmed me and shook my hand and gave me hugs. The musicians started playing and the choir sang, "So glad you're here!" Now, I was *truly* suspicious. I was not used to this. I was fresh off the street. So, anytime someone hugged me, I knew they wanted something. I was trained that anyone who shook your hand was not your friend. Most people who knew me did not want me around. I was grimy; I was a thief; I was callous and borderline ruthless. My momma told me that one of my teachers told her, "Every time he walks through the door, it's like a bad toothache." That is why I had no contact with family and had no real friends. People did not trust me. Yet, on a Sunday a little after eight in the morning, total strangers were happy to see me. I cried. About an hour later, a preacher walked out to the platform. I later learned his name: Bishop Glen A. Staples. After he preached his sermon, he opened the doors of the church and he invited people to receive Jesus, to be candidates for baptism, or to become members of the church. I did not want to do any of those things.

I knew I needed to, but there was no way I would walk up to the front. A woman standing beside me told me to "Go on up there."

I replied, "No, I'm all right."

Then the preacher waited a few more minutes (although it felt like hours) and he kept pulling, pleading, and asking. Then the same woman nudged me again. I later learned her name was Mother Cary. She asked, "You want me to go with ya?"

I finally said, "Okay." Mother Cary took me by the hand and walked me down the aisle. The people clapped their hands and praised God. Several of us were taken to the back room of the church. A minister in the room gave us some instructions and read from Romans 10:9-10: "That if thou shalt confess with thy mouth the Lord Jesus, and shalt believe in thine heart that God hath raised him from the dead, thou shalt be saved. For with the heart man believeth unto righteousness; and with the mouth confession is made unto salvation" (AKJV). Then he led us in prayer to receive Christ.

# True Prosperity

———•✦•———

True prosperity begins when a person believes and receives the Lord Jesus Christ into his or her life. When we hear the words "success" and "prosperity", we immediately think of money and having material things, but that is backward. A person's life does not consist of the abundance of possessions (Luke 12:15, NIV).

I did not say you should not or could not have things; I'm saying things do not make you or define you. The true measure of a man is based upon his relationship with God. Jesus Himself said, "What does it profit a man to gain the whole world and forfeit his soul?" (Mark 8:36-37, NIV). Your soul is so precious to God that nothing but the precious blood of Jesus could save you (1 Peter 1:18-19). Think about it: if money could save you, wouldn't God have used it? Who has more money than God? The "cattle upon a thousand hills belong to Him" (Psalm 50:10). " 'The silver is mine and the gold is mine,' saith the Lord" (Haggai 2:8). The earth is the Lord's and everything in it (Psalm 24:1). Revelation 21 speaks of a city of pure gold, pearls, and precious stones. God does not have a money problem. If anybody could have purchased your redemption with money, it would have been God.

He loves you so much and values your soul so much that nothing but the precious blood of Jesus could save your soul. When God wanted to rescue you, He did not look at His bank account; He looked to Jesus (John 3:16). True prosperity begins on the inside.

**Prayer of Salvation**

At this present time, I have a vibrant relationship with God. I have a successful radio and television ministry with an average of 1,000,000 listeners in the US* alone. The psychologist who said I needed to be on medication told me I no longer needed it. The doctor told me I was lucky to be alive. She said, "I thought at the least you would have to have a breathing apparatus." At my seasonal check-up she exclaimed, "Excellent!"

I no longer sleep on a park bench; I live in a house. I no longer live a promiscuous life style; I am happily married and faithful to one woman. Glory to God! I no longer have to steal clothing from department stores and wash my body in public bathrooms. My closet is full of fine suits and clothing. I am the top producer on my job with a six-figure household. I am a licensed real estate agent, and I manage the most successful branch in the company. My minister's license has the names of Bishop Glen A. Staples, Bishop T.D. Jakes, and Bishop Sherman Watkins on it. I am one hundred percent debt-free and now I am a successful author.

I am the same guy many folks said would not make it. They said I would always be a crack head. They said I was crazy, a jailbird, and a nobody. One lady flat-out told me I was a loser! Well, take a look at me now. I gave my life to Jesus, and He gave me a brand new life. God spared my life. He did not allow me to die in the street. I was spared from a life in prison. My lifestyle called for jail and hell, but God pardoned me.

My friend, the Bible declares Jesus Christ is the same yesterday, today and forever (Hebrews 13:8) and He does not show favoritism (Acts 10:34). What He did for me, He will do for you. Before we go any further, we need to settle this: there is no true success outside of a relationship with Jesus Christ.

True prosperity begins when a person believes the glorious Gospel of Jesus Christ. How "God so loved the world (and that includes you), that He gave His only begotten Son, that whosoever (that is you) believes on Him should not perish, but have everlasting life" (John 3:16). Jesus came to seek and to save that which was lost. He bore your sin on the Cross. He suffered in your place. He was despised and rejected, beaten and whipped. He was nailed to the cross as a sacrifice for your sin. He bled and He died to purchase your freedom. He lay in the grave for three days and nights, but on the third day, He rose from the dead. Romans 10:9-10 says: "That if thou shalt confess with thy mouth the Lord Jesus, and shalt believe in thine heart that God hath raised him from the dead, thou shalt be saved. For with the heart man believeth unto righteousness; and with the mouth confession is made unto salvation." Do you believe that? Then say this prayer with me: "God, I believe Jesus is the Christ, He bore my sin on the cross and He died for my sin, He was buried and was raised from the dead on the third day. I accept His sacrifice and humbly confess Jesus is my Lord." Congratulations! Hallelujah! I join the angels in heaven in celebrating your return back to God. The Bible says: "there is joy in heaven in the presence of the angels of God over one sinner that repents" (Luke 15:10).

Now, I want you to do three things: 1) Get yourself a Holy Bible, 2) Go tell someone that you made Jesus the Lord of your life, and 3) Get yourself into a Bible-believing church. I will talk about the importance of these three things later. For now, reading your Bible and going to church are your connections to success. When a child is born, he needs to be cared for and nourished until he grows up and can care for himself. Your Bible is your food and your church is the guardian that Jesus ordained to raise you up. Remember this: there is no true success outside of the Bible and going to church. I want to share a scripture with you before we talk about how to grow with God. Proverbs 4:18 reads: "But the path of the just *is* as the shining light, that shineth more and more unto the perfect day."

There is no such thing as an "overnight success". Success is a process. When you accepted Jesus as your Lord, you started down a path. Things will begin to get better and brighter as you gain knowledge of God and act on His Word. The God kind of success is not an accident or automatic. The God kind of success is accessed as you actively engage in and habitually practice spiritual laws. Jesus said to the people who believed on Him, "If you continue in my word [emphasis is on "continue"], then [the word "then" implies a sequence] are you my disciples indeed, and you shall know the truth, and the truth shall make you free" (John 8:30-32.) If all we had to do was believe, we could have it made; but notice the words: "If," "continue," "*then*," "are ye my disciples indeed," and, "free." Between "many believed on Him" (v. 30) and "free" (v. 32), there is obviously a process.

In order to access success through God, it is imperative we become students of the Word (2 Timothy 2:15). In order for success to flow, there must be a "word flow". Successful people are disciplined people. Discipline yourself to sit at the Master's feet. Lean on the Holy Spirit, listen to your pastor, and learn to flow with God. There is rhythm to success through God. In this book, I am going to show you how to get in step with that rhythm.

# The Success Flow

After prayer one morning, as I got up off my knees, I heard these words: "The Success Flow." After proper praying, my spiritual ears are normally receptive to the voice of the Lord. I know it was from the Lord, but I had no clue what it meant. I wrote the words down in a little book I keep on the nightstand beside my bed. I knew it was not time yet, because I did not know anything about it, nor was I prompted by the Holy Spirit.

Some months later, I got the green light. In other words, the Holy Spirit prompted me to go forward. Being a student of the Word, I got my study tools and went to work. Here is what I found in Joshua 1:1-9, Psalm 1:1-3, and 3 John 1:1-4:

> Joshua 1:1-9:
> Now after the death of Moses the servant of the LORD it came to pass, that the LORD spake unto Joshua the son of Nun, Moses' minister, saying, "Moses my servant is dead; now therefore arise, go over this Jordan, thou, and all this people, unto

the land which I do give to them, *even* to the children of Israel. Every place that the sole of your foot shall tread upon, that have I given unto you, as I said unto Moses. From the wilderness and this Lebanon even unto the great river, the river Euphrates, all the land of the Hittites, and unto the great sea toward the going down of the sun, shall be your coast. There shall not any man be able to stand before thee all the days of thy life: as I was with Moses, *so* I will be with thee: I will not fail thee, nor forsake thee. Be strong and of a good courage: for unto this people shalt thou divide for an inheritance the land, which I sware unto their fathers to give them. Only be thou strong and very courageous, that thou mayest observe to do according to all the law, which Moses my servant commanded thee: turn not from it *to* the right hand or *to* the left, that thou mayest prosper whithersoever thou goest. This book of the law shall not depart out of thy mouth; but thou shalt meditate therein day and night, that thou mayest observe to do according to all that is written therein: for then thou shalt make thy way prosperous, and then thou shalt have good success. Have not I commanded thee? Be strong and of a good courage; be not afraid, neither be thou dismayed: for the LORD thy God *is* with thee whithersoever thou goest."

Psalm 1:1-3:
Blessed *is* the man that walketh not in the counsel of the ungodly, nor standeth in the way of sinners, nor sitteth in the seat of the scornful. But his delight *is* in the law of the LORD; and in his law doth he meditate day and night. And he shall be like a tree planted by the rivers of water, that bringeth forth his fruit in his season; his leaf also shall not wither; and whatsoever he doeth shall prosper.

3 John 1: 1-4:
The elder unto the well beloved Gaius, whom I love in the truth. Beloved, I wish above all things that thou mayest prosper and be in health, even as thy soul prospereth. For I rejoiced greatly, when the brethren came and testified of the truth that is in thee, even as thou walkest in the truth. I have no greater joy than to hear that my children walk in truth.

I encourage you to meditate, memorize, and maintain Joshua 1:8, Psalm 1:1-3, and 3 John chapter 9. These scriptures teach you how to train your soul. When most people hear the words "success" or "prosperity", they immediately think of money or materials things.

Have you noticed I have not said a word about money? Later on I will, because there is no such thing as prosperity without money. Never confuse the process. You have to become wealthy on the inside before you can become wealthy on the outside. The Apostle John said, "I desire above all things that you prosper and be in health, even as your soul prospers." In other words, your health and wealth are in direct proportion to the condition of your soul. When things are not going well on the outside, the first thing to ask yourself is, "What is going on inside?" Then, tell yourself: "I am going to have to get my soul well, if I am going to be truly successful."

**Success**

Let's define terms here. At least a million people will read this book. Because we are all on different levels, and have various backgrounds, we have different ideas about success. What one person calls success, another person calls mediocre. To make sure we are on the same page as we study together here, let me share with you what I mean when I say success I mean to excel to the highest place in any endeavor or thing desired. I am not just talking about accomplishing your goals, but excelling, surpassing, ,and being superior in your God ordained purpose. I did not say to compare yourself to other people or try to be better than other people. I am talking about excelling in your arena, your field, and your vocation. This means doing what God has called you to do, and doing it extremely well. Let us look at what God told Joshua in Joshua 1:8: "This book of the law shall not depart out of thy mouth; but thou shalt meditate therein day and night, that thou mayest observe to do according to all that is written therein: for then thou shalt make thy way prosperous, and then thou shalt have good success."

Isn't it interesting that God uses the words "good success"? What is good success? Before you answer that question, keep in mind the Bible is an Eastern book. The Old Testament was written in Hebrew and God spoke those words to a Jewish man. So let us answer the question from that perspective and then see how it applies to us today. When you study it in Hebrew you will find words like "wisdom," "prudence," and "circumspect" to have insight. In fact, some Bible versions translated it that way. For example: "And then you shall deal wisely and have good success" (Amplified). I like to say it this way: "To have insight and understanding in the affairs of life."

Now, please listen carefully to what I am about to say. We have been robbed! All we ever hear is "get a good education," "get a good job," "get a good career," "get a good skill," "get a good woman," "get a good man," "get a good this," and "get a good that."

When was the last time someone told you "get good success"? Joshua had a daunting task in front of him: to take Moses' place! Are you serious, Lord? Deuteronomy 34:10-12 reads:

> And there arose not a prophet since in Israel like unto Moses, whom the LORD knew face to face, in all the signs and the wonders, which the LORD sent him to do in the land of Egypt to Pharaoh, and to all his servants, and to all his land, and in all that mighty hand, and in all the great terror which Moses shewed in the sight of all Israel.

Folks, Moses was a tough act to follow. Even if Joshua did have a good education, he was not going to lead a few million people into the Promised Land based on his own wits. The walls of Jericho did not fall down because Joshua had a good career, good skills, or good looks (Joshua 6). Now, do not misunderstand me. I strongly encourage you to go to school, educate yourself, get a skillset, and get life skills and training, but I would be robbing you if that were all I told you. The kind of success I am talking about is not in a textbook, nor will you go to a department store and get it out of a glass case.

The success God speaks of is a supernatural thing. It is not all God and it's not all me. It is God and me, working together, working jointly. The Success Flow is a heaven and earth connection. In the book of Genesis, Adam and God worked together. God created the garden and turned it over to the man. God planted a garden then turned it over to the man to cultivate it (Genesis 2:15). God formed every beast of the ground and every fowl of the air, and then turned it over to man. Adam's part was to name every creature (Genesis 2:19). They had a heaven and earth connection. Adam was designed and equipped to have dominion and subdue the earth, the same way God rules in the heavens (Genesis 1:26-28). Jesus told the disciples to pray: "thy kingdom come, thy will be done on earth, as it is in heaven" (Matthew 6:10).

Then again in Matthew 18:18, Jesus said whatever we "bind on earth is bound in heaven," and whatever we "loose on earth is loosed in heaven." Can you see the heaven and earth connection? It is supposed to be God and you working together. God never intended for you to live life independently of Him. He wants you to get a revelation that it is in Him you live and move and have your being (Acts 17:28).

So yes, get your education, get your skillset, improve yourself, and use common sense, but do not forget the supernatural. Trust in the Lord; lean hard on Him. Put His Word in your mouth and on your mind until it gets in your heart and programs you for success. You will eventually get to a place where you make divinely directed decisions. God will show you how to maneuver through the vicissitudes of life, including showing how to use your education properly, how to manage your resources, run your business, and even teach you how to manage your emotions.

Your decisions will no longer be according to a textbook, but God's book.

### All Things are Possible

As I meditated one morning, I asked myself, *how is that possible? How can a person prosper wherever he goes or in whatever he does? What about my pedigree? What about my family history? My juvenile record? My criminal record? I made a mess back there, Lord, and I burned a lot of bridges, and hurt a lot of people emotionally. Dear God, my family does not even want anything to do with me.* That is when I heard these words register in my spirit: "With God, all things are possible." Then I was lead to Mark 10:27, "And Jesus looking upon them saith, 'With men *it is* impossible, but not with God: for with God all things are possible.' "

To the natural mind, that sounds unfathomable. In my mind, that is hard to comprehend. If I had to do it on my own, that would be impossible, but not with God. Remember two things: 1) It is a supernatural thing and 2) With God, anything can happen. Say this out loud: "Anything can happen." Say it again: "Anything can happen." Now, let me ask you a few questions: Does the word "anything" include success? Does the word "anything" include a prosperous marriage? How about a successful business? What about a flourishing ministry? Does "anything" include freedom from sickness? Do not choke on me now. I asked does "anything" include freedom from sickness? What about being debt-free? Now, remember, you are not going to accomplish this on your own; it is a heaven and earth connection, a supernatural thing. Get your eyes off yourself, your inadequacies, your insufficiencies, and your human reasoning. With men, it is impossible, but not with God, for with God, anything can happen. I would like you to begin to say two things to yourself and meditate on them for a few days:

1. With God anything can happen.

2. God can get anything to me, from anywhere, through anybody, at any time.

**Get with God**

One key factor to getting in the "success flow" is to get "with God," or let us say it this way: "get with the God of impossibilities." When I was sworn in after I joined the military in the early 1980s, I was in a room full of other men and woman. We had to raise our right hands and solemnly swear or affirm we would support and defend the Constitution of the United States of America against all enemies. Then I was put on an airplane and sent to boot camp. Why did they send me to basic training? I already promised I would support and defend. You mean to tell me my promise was not enough? I thought after my pledge, I was in the Army. I was, but the Army was not in me. I had to learn the Army's ways. How to march to the Army's drum, how the Army thinks, how the Army talks; in other words, I was in the Army, but now it was time to get "with the Army".

Before I joined the military, my friends teased me and said, "They are going to brainwash you." What did they mean? The Army would elicit a radical change in my ideas and beliefs. The military knew in order for me to be successful they would have to change my pattern of thinking. There would have to be a paradigm shift; I could no longer think like a civilian. I had to get with the Army's program in order to be successful.

The same is true with us believers. When we believed in our hearts and confessed with our mouths that Jesus is Lord, we were instantly delivered out of the control of darkness and translated into the Kingdom of God's dear Son (Colossians 1:13). Now, we must learn to operate by Kingdom principles if we are to get Kingdom results and flow in the God's kind of success.

One key factor to getting in the "success flow" is to get "with God." John 1:1-3 tells us: "In the beginning was the Word, and the Word was with God, and the Word was God. The same was in the beginning with God. All things were made by him; and without him was not any thing made that was made."

You get "with God" by getting with His Word. There is no success flow if there is no word flow. The Word was "with God" in the beginning and all things were made by the Word. If your are going to walk in God's kind of success, it is important to connect with the Word of God from the beginning and create a successful environment with your words.

Let us look again at Joshua 1:8: "This book of the law shall not depart out of thy mouth; but thou shalt meditate therein day and night, that thou mayest observe to do according to all that is written therein: for then thou shalt make thy way prosperous, and then thou shalt have good success." As I meditated on this verse one morning, I asked the Lord, "Lord, why did you tell Joshua to put the word in his mouth?"

He answered me immediately, "Your success is in your mouth."

That made sense to me because I knew death and life are in the power of my tongue (Proverbs 18:21). If death and life are in the power of the tongue, then so are success and failure. Blessing and cursing are in the power of the tongue (James 3:10).

Read this next verse carefully in Deuteronomy 30:19: "I call heaven and earth to record this day against you, *that* I have set before you life and death, blessing and cursing: therefore choose life, that both thou and thy seed may live." Notice the children of Israel had a choice to make: life or death, blessing or cursing. The only way to make that choice is with words. Write this next statement down, highlight it, mark it, tweet it, put it on Facebook—do something with it. Ready? Success is a choice. Say this out loud three times: "I choose to be successful! I choose to be successful! I choose to be successful!"

Make a quality decision to never talk defeat or failure ever again. Right after the Lord told me that success was in my mouth, I immediately said to Him, "The next thing you said was 'meditate on the word day and night.' Why did you tell Joshua to put it on his mind?"

The Lord again answered quickly: "success is a mindset."

**Listen to this Prophecy**

When you speak my Word and meditate on it regularly, you are programming yourself for success. The more you mediate on that which is written and the more you mediate on that which is said as one shall speak under the anointing and inspiration of the Spirit. Then, little by little, it will become real to you, on the inside of you, in your spirit, in your inner man. That word will take shape and form as a babe is formed in the womb. As it is written: "Until Christ be formed in you" (Galatians 4:19). You will then grow and become strong and able to do the works I called you to do. Lean not on your own understanding. What I called you to do cannot be done on your own wits; you will need my help, my grace, and my ability. Connect with me. If you will abide in me and my words abide in you, I will see to it that no matter where you go or whatever you do, you prosper, saith the Lord.

The Apostle Paul told Timothy to give his attention to the Word of God to mediate on it and give himself completely to it, so that his profiting (or his success) may appear to all (2 Timothy 4:13-16).

**Mary Got with God**

Let's examine Luke 1:26-38:

> And in the sixth month the angel Gabriel was sent from God unto a city of Galilee, named Nazareth, to a virgin espoused to a man whose name was Joseph, of the house of David; and the virgin's name *was* Mary. And the angel came in unto her, and said, "Hail, *thou that art* highly favoured, the Lord *is* with thee: blessed *art* thou among women." And when she saw *him*, she was troubled at his saying, and cast in her mind what manner of salutation this should be. And the

angel said unto her, "Fear not, Mary: for thou hast found favour with God. And, behold, thou shalt conceive in thy womb, and bring forth a son, and shalt call his name JESUS. He shall be great, and shall be called the Son of the Highest: and the Lord God shall give unto him the throne of his father David: and he shall reign over the house of Jacob for ever; and of his kingdom there shall be no end." Then said Mary unto the angel, "How shall this be, seeing I know not a man?" And the angel answered and said unto her, "The Holy Ghost shall come upon thee, and the power of the Highest shall overshadow thee: therefore also that holy thing which shall be born of thee shall be called the Son of God. And, behold, thy cousin Elisabeth, she hath also conceived a son in her old age: and this is the sixth month with her, who was called barren. For with God nothing shall be impossible." And Mary said, "Behold the handmaid of the Lord; be it unto me according to thy word." And the angel departed from her.

In the natural, it would have been impossible for Mary to conceive a child without a man. When she got with the God of impossibilities, the unfathomable became possible. How did Mary get with God? The answer is in verse 38: "be it unto me according to thy word." Mary believed the Word of the Lord, agreed, and connected. Beloved, the success flow is a "Holy thing;" it is supernatural. When you determine to put God's Word in your mouth, meditate on it and put it into practice, the Holy Ghost will come upon you and the power of the Highest will overshadow you; a Holy thing will be conceived in the womb of your spirit. In time, you will give birth to God's kind of success. Say this out loud: "Father, you desire for me to prosper, and be in health, even as my soul prospers. Be it unto me according to thy Word."

The God of impossibilities was "with Moses" and He was "with Joshua" (Joshua 1:5). He also promised to be "with you always, even unto the end of the world" (Matthew 28:20). Never underestimate the importance of getting with God. Remember, you get with God by getting with His Word. In order for success to flow, the Word must flow. It must flow from your mouth, flow through your mind, flow from your heart, and permeate your entire lifestyle. Simply put: the Word of God must be a vital part of your life.

**Declaration:** The God of impossibilities is with me, therefore I can prosper wherever I go, and in whatever I do I can flow in success.

# Prerequisites – Process – Principles

There are certain things that are required of you before you can walk in the God kind of success. Success without integrity will kill you.

Your success in life is for a purpose. Always remember: your success is supposed to flow. Everything God did for you and in you is an investment for the advancement of the Kingdom. Train yourself to be Kingdom-minded. As you climb the ladder of success, keep in mind every step and every stage is Kingdom related. Every level and every stage will require you to be even more focused on the Father's business.

If God doesn't have your heart, He certainly will not have your hand. Take a look at the parable in Luke 12:16-21. This rich man came to a place where "success brought him excess." The Bible says he thought within himself and said, "the only problem was his thinking and speaking were not in line with God's Word." He had access to Joshua 1:8, and he had access to Psalm 1:1-3. He had access to Proverbs and Ecclesiastes. If the law of the Lord were his meditation and delight, he would have known to tithe, sow seed, and give to the poor.

The un-renewed mind is extremely self-centered. Notice how many times he said, "I," or "I do," "I have," "will I do," "I will pull down," or, "I will bestow." It was all about him. He had no concept of the success flow. Please always keep in mind your success in life is not all about *you*. Every accomplishment, every promotion, everything in the arena of success is Kingdom-related. If you train yourself to be Kingdom-minded, you will instinctively know the excess of success is Kingdom-related. Did you get that?

In other words, success is supposed to flow (Proverbs 1:32). The word simple in that verse means naïve, foolish, or ignorant. If you don't know the purpose of success, it will destroy you. God couldn't make me rich if I was still addicted to crack cocaine. I would have been like the rich man in Luke 12. "What shall I do? I will rent a room and call an escort service. I will get a bunch of cocaine, booze, and Viagra and say, 'It's your thing, do what you wanna do.' " God would have said the same thing to me that He said to the rich man: "You Fool!" Say this out loud: The excess of my success is to invest in the Father's business.

To keep us from destroying ourselves, our Father has designed for us to go through a process—a heavenly curriculum. In other words, there are some things that we must experience, some spiritual classes we must take, and lessons that we must learn. Particularly in the area of money, make no question about it; you must pass the money test. There is no true success to the non-tither. There is no success to the non-sower. There is no true success to the non-giver. Money cannot be your God. You're going to have to choose this day whom you will serve. No man can serve two masters, for either he will hate the one and love the other, or he will hold to the one and despise the other. You cannot serve God and mammon ( Matthew 6:24 KJV).

The word "mammon" is the Aramaic word for riches, money, and wealth; it is sometimes personified as a false God or an object of worship. It is often regarded as an evil influence. So it's not the money that's the problem; it's the evil influence or the demon spirit that has such a hold on an individual who has the money.

He becomes consumed with himself. He doesn't want to tithe; he doesn't want to help anybody outside of his small circle. Money has become his God. Tithing, sowing, and honoring God with your income is your declaration before heaven and earth that God is your source. The only way to break the power of the spirit of mammon is to sow. You can pray, rebuke the Devil, shout, and confess all you want. Yet, when you get done, you will always hear Jesus say, "Sow" Please take a moment and read Luke 8:1-3.

After I gave my life to the Lord, I was so grateful. Somewhere deep inside my heart, I wanted to give. I know exactly how those women felt. They were so grateful for what Jesus had done for them. The text doesn't say Jesus asked them for anything. They supported Him from their own resources willingly. So when I surrendered my life to Jesus, I wanted everybody to be delivered, too. I wanted the church to stay open. I wanted the lights on and the bills paid. I didn't want anybody to come to the Temple of Praise and find the doors were closed because we didn't pay the bills.

I knew dozens of people who were like me right in the same neighborhood; they were drug addicts, dealers, streetwalkers, and gang members—all hurting, all suffering, and all bound. I knew if they could get into this building, they could get some help. I wanted to do my part. The only problem was, I was broke. I prayed and cried before God because inside my heart was a burning desire to help, but I had no money.

One day, these words came to my ears: "empty yourself." I don't know how I understood those words, but I did. He required me to meet certain conditions. Deep inside, I had other issues to deal with, deep-seated issues.

The Psalmist in Psalm 19:12 cried out, "cleanse me from my secret faults." God wanted my heart, my devotion, and my obedience. He didn't want my money—he wanted me! He knew if He had my heart, He could have my hand. My love for Him would compel me to give. So my prayer was, "Lord, I want to give," and His reply was, "empty yourself." *Give up your ways for my ways. Give up your thoughts for my thoughts. Give up your agenda. Give up your heathen street mentality. Surrender and empty yourself. Decrease so I can increase.* Glory to God! One songwriter put it perfectly: "My life is not my own, to you I belong. I give myself, I give myself to You." Once you meet that prerequisite, giving is no problem.

God is a God of first things first. He's a God of principle. He watches your agenda, your motives, and your heart. He always wants you to be aware of what's going on inside of yourself. Never forget: God is Holy. He wants you to form a sanctified heart. An unsanctified heart cannot handle the God of success. My desire to give was noble, but my hidden desires polluted my heart's desire. Only a clean heart could offer a clean sacrifice to God. Remember, when I met Jesus, I had more then just a money problem. I had a myriad of issues. Beloved, you're not going to watch dozens of pornographic films, live a promiscuous lifestyle, and sleep in numerous crack houses and jailhouses and indulge in the street life and come out unscathed. When you received Jesus as Lord, He recreated your spirit, but now something has to be done with your soul and with your body.

> "And the very God of peace sanctify you wholly; and I pray God your whole spirit and soul and body be preserved blameless unto the coming of our Lord Jesus Christ" (1 Thessalonians 5:23 KJV).

Notice what the desire of your Heavenly Father is: "for you to be sanctified wholly." In order for you to fully understand the Father's desire, let's take this verse apart. Let's begin with the word, "peace".

According to *Strong's Hebrew Lexicon*, both in Hebrew and in Greek, "peace" is defined as your entire welfare. This includes financial prosperity, health, safety, deliverance from evil and wholeness, completeness, rest, and my favorite: "to set at one again."

Sin had devastated my soul—my mind, my will, my emotions, every part of me. Spiritually, I was dead. My soul was scarred, damaged, and programmed by lust and corruption. My physical body was sick and malnourished. Financially, I was broke; I was in debt and my credit was horrible. My relationships with people and family were entirely abnormal. I was born-again, but Jesus wasn't satisfied with only saving my soul; He wanted to make me whole.. He wanted to set me at one again.

Let me say it another way: *My child, I began work in you, but I'm not finished. I need you to get back everything that you lost: Your money, your relationships, your health, and your pride. Your dignity and your self-respect. Everything. I am the God of peace (wholeness) and not the God of part or some. My earnest, heartfelt desire is for you to prosper and be in health, even as your soul prospers. The process I started in you needs to flow through you and out of you. Success must flow.*

**Translate – Mediate – Activate**

As we take this verse apart, I want to share with you a study of principle I learned from The Holy Ghost. It's called translate, meditate, and activate. You begin by taking the word that grabs your interest. If and when you encounter a word you don't understand, please take the time to look it up. Take the word that appeals to you and look it up in a good Bible concordance—personally I found *Strong's Concordance* and *W.E. Vines Expository Dictionary* to be extremely helpful (Dr. Strong and Dr. Vines have already done the work for you). As I stated earlier, the Bible is an Eastern book, so it helps to look at it in its original language. Once you have the word translated, begin to meditate. Just quietly begin to roll the information around in your mind and mutter to yourself. Read the verse again and get quiet before the Lord. Don't be a prisoner to one translation of the Bible. Be a student of the Word.

Among other things, meditation gives birth to revelation. According to Joshua 1:8, meditation is a prerequisite to good success. After you meditate, it's time to activate. You activate God's word with corresponding action. Faith always speaks and acts upon what it believes. After you translate and meditate, you activate the words by speaking out what you've learned. You also act on the revelations that you've received. You translate to get information. You meditate to get revelation. You activate for application.

I will give you an opportunity to practice this study principle shortly. Let's finish by extracting more information from 1 Thessalonians 5:23. The word sanctify means to set apart. The Father wants our entire being cleansed and dedicated to Him. The final word we will look at is "Wholly". It simply means to be complete through and through. When we put all this information together, it becomes clear the God of Peace (wholeness) wants us to be complete—like Him! There is no bypassing the process. The road to God's kind of success must be traveled.

If you live in Washington, DC, and you want to travel to New York, there is a certain course you must follow. It doesn't matter if you take a plane, a train, or a bus. It doesn't matter if you drive your own vehicle. There is only one direction: north. If you're going to walk in the God kind of success, there are certain prerequisites you must meet. A process you have to go through. There are Kingdom principles we must follow.

I am finding out there are least three tests we must pass in order for God's kind of success to flow: the money test, the faith test, and the sanctification test. These tests will ensure we will remain men and women of purpose and principle. They enable us to keep our priorities straight. Successful people don't do what they want to do, think the way they want to think, and say whatever they feel like saying. They adhere to God's spiritual laws and they follow a Kingdom code of conduct. They maintain a certain level of honor and integrity.

Okay, it's time to activate; say this out loud: Heavenly Father, I submit to your earnest desire to make me whole. Thank you for the work that you began in me. I yield to the Holy Spirit and allow what you started to flow. Flow through my spirit, flow through my soul. Flow through my body, flow in my finances, flow in my relationships. Let the Spirit flow. Let the love flow, and let the Word flow. Sanctify me through and through. Thank you for preserving me blameless unto the coming of my Lord, Jesus Christ. Amen.

The process we go through not only sets us at one again, but it unveils a truth that will be a guiding force for the rest of our lives. That truth is this: I must be successful if I'm to advance the Kingdom of God. My decisions must be Kingdom related. My success, my influence, my position in the earth realm must be guided by Kingdom purpose. There's too much at stake. There are souls in the balance. Failure is not an option. I have to be successful. Once this revelation dawns on our spirit, we begin to live on purpose.

**My Personal Money Test**

**Take a moment and read Mark 12:41-44.**

After I received the revelation to empty myself, I went and got what money I had, which was a few dollars in change, mostly pennies. I put them in an offering envelope and wrapped it with tape. The weight was more than the envelope could bear. At the next church service, I dropped it in the basket. I was humbled. Honestly, I was a bit embarrassed. My mind wondered what the deacon would think when the weighty offering hit the bottom of the basket. Deep inside, all I heard was, "Empty yourself." It's not the size of your offering; it's a matter of trust, love, and obedience. If the heart is not right, the money means nothing. Verse 41 says Jesus noticed "how they cast money into the treasury." How they did it—I'll say it again until you fully absorb it—how they cast their money in. God wants to know how. What's your motive? Is this a ritual? Are you giving out of a cheerful heart? How are you giving? Notice Jesus sat by the treasury, not the pulpit, or the choir, but by the money. Never forget the words of the Lord Jesus Christ: "For where your treasure is, there will your heart also be." He sat by the treasury because the location of your "treasure" reveals your heart.

## The Success Flow

Not long after I sowed my widow's mite, I landed a good job. I was a marketing agent in the DC metropolitan area. I had no experience whatsoever. I helped a friend out with her business. She paid me chump change for gathering information at one of her sites, otherwise known as lead generation.

One day while working a site in National Harbor, Maryland, I noticed an older lady watching me. She stood about twenty feet away and she kept watching me. I thought maybe she's some type of inspector for the company, or maybe she thought I was good looking; I had no idea. Finally, she walked up to me, pointed her finger at me and said, "They aren't paying you what you're worth. You should be making a $100,000 a year." She rattled on for a few minutes. As she talked, I did the math. I thought to myself, *if she's half right, that's $50,000 a year,* which was way more than I made then and there. Long story short, I accepted her offer. One month later, I was the lead generation operations manager. A few months after that, I was a marketing manager. Not long after that, I had her job! Glory to God! It started with the widow's mite. I then became a consistent tither. Now I'm a bona fide sower.

I thoroughly enjoyed my job. Please forgive me if this sounds arrogant, but I was darn good at it! Some of the pros even told me I was a freak of nature. They couldn't figure me out. Before I became the boss, my trainer, Steve Ingram —who was a pro among pros—and the senior manager came to me one day. He pulled out a schedule and said, "Geren, we've noticed you're only working a few days a week, but you're making more money than anyone else. We were wondering if you could pick up a few more shifts."

From a business point-of-view, I understood his thought process: "If we can get him to work more, he'll make more money for us." So, I picked up more work. As I worked, I'd sing praises and preach right out in the open air. I would preach my bishop's sermons. I'd copy him to a tee. Some people thought that I was crazy; others laughed. I kept on praising and preaching. And I kept on getting promoted. Glory to God!

One day while in church, my assistant pastor filled in for the bishop who was on assignment. He stood on the steps of the pulpit and said, "This church should have been paid off." I was stunned. I thought it had already been paid. He then went on to tell us how the bishop's tithe was well over ten percent, and the bishop was the biggest tither in the church. I thought, *dear God, what can I do? I want to be the biggest tither too.* I then prayed at the pew, "Lord, I want to pay off your church." I had no clue how much it was, but with the size of the church I guessed it was a lot.

I went home with an unshakable burden for the house of my God. I thought about it a lot. I prayed about it. I meditated and tried to figure out how I would get the money. One Sunday service, they made an announcement that the church needed three hundred saints to pledge five hundred dollars toward our yearly Holy Convocation. The Spirit of the Lord promoted me to start by being one of those three hundred. I walked up to the head deacon and I said, "I want to be one of the three hundred." He gave me instructions and I went back to my seat.

A few days later, I awoke one morning and as soon as my feet hit the floor, I heard that voice again. This time, He said, "I want you to give ten thousand dollars to the church."

Without even thinking, or blinking, I immediately answered, "Yes, Lord." As is my custom, I went into prayer. Then I had my coffee and my study time. There are two things I never do: I never let a day go by without praising His name, and I never leave the house without getting in the Word. Success in life hinges on hearing from God. I don't look at any texts, emails, or voicemails until after I read my Bible. I don't even like talking to humans before I spend time with Him. My wife is the only one to whom I will speak, and that's to say good morning. Other than that, nobody comes before my morning with my Savior.

I need to hear from God the way a door needs hinges. If you remove the hinges from the door, it will fall. It has to be connected to the hinges in order to serve its purpose. I have discovered without spending time with Him, I fall apart. I can't hold up. I don't flow right. "I need you, O Lord. In you I live and move and have my being." Glory to His name! Blessed is the person who recognizes that without Him, I am nothing!

After my study time, I proceed to the gym. I workout four to five times a week. Successful people take care of their health. While working out, I stopped and said, "Lord, was that you who told me to give ten thousand dollars to the church? You see, even though I said yes, Lord, there was one major problem: I don't have ten thousand dollars."

I thought about that all morning, but I didn't say anything to anybody—not my wife, or the Lord. I just thought about it. Do you remember when God told Abraham to offer up Isaac? The Bible says he rose up early in the morning, and three days later he saw the place that God had told him to go to (Genesis 22:3). He had three days to think about that. He had to reckon, consider, and calculate. He thought about it like you and me.

He had three days to figure it out. He finally came to the conclusion: God's obviously going to raise his child from the dead (Hebrews 11:19)! As I thought about what the Lord told me, I finally asked Him, "Was that you Lord who told me to give ten thousand to the church?"

Instantly, He replied, "Would the Devil tell you to give ten thousand dollars to the church?"

That was the end of that conversation. I knew it was the will of the Lord. It was testing time. He called me higher. There was more that He required of me. It was time to test my faith. I was already a tither. I was already a sower. Now it was time to test me. I still had a money problem. I was in debt. I owed the government, the hospital, and the taxman. I had six accounts in default and in collections. In reality, I needed that money. I still had bills and I planned on getting married. I had a choice to make. Do the logical thing, or obey God?

As soon as I put my feet on the floor the next morning, the voice of God came to me again, saying, "Give your whole check to the church."

Again, I instantly replied, "Yes, Lord."

I didn't know it at that time, but in retrospect, I can say He trained me. He personally walked me through the process. Beloved, I'm not sure it will make sense to you, but I pray it will be revealed to you.

**Giving is Spiritual**

Your giving connects you to God's system: God's laws and principles of finance, God's economy, God's way of doing things. Always remember God is a spirit. He's not going to get up off the throne, come down, and hand you a check from the Bank of Heaven. He works in the unseen world of the spirit. Every time you tithe, every time you sow, a spiritual transaction has taken place. You have opened up an account with God, and in return He will meet all your needs according to His resources in heavenly places.

**Divinely – Directed – Decisions**

When He told me to give my whole check to the church, He unfolded a strategy to make the $10,000 pledge good. He knew I was in debt. He knew I had bills. He knew the exact date I would get married. He knew I was a tither and a sower. He also knew the end of a thing from the beginning (Isaiah 46:10). I was the one who did not know. I was the one who did not understand. I had to trust Him. I didn't borrow money or beg for it. I didn't try to manipulate people or devise a scheme. I followed Joshua 1:8. I put His word in my mouth. I meditated and I put the word into action. I now made divinely directed decisions.

At the next church service, when it was offering time, I put my tithe in the box and another portion of my check in the general offering. I also sowed a love offering in the basket designed for the pastor. I walked over to the side of the pulpit where a minister received pledges from the three hundred.

I said, "I am one of the three hundred."

She smiled and said, "Praise the Lord!" She took my name and a portion of my pledge in cash. Then I told her, "I want to make another pledge."

She said, "Okay," and then she asked how much.

I said, "Ten thousand dollars."

She said, "Praise the Lord, ten dollars."

I said, "No, ten *thousand* dollars."

Her eyes lit up and she said in surprise, "Oh . . . well, praise the Lord!" She wrote down my pledge and I walked away.

The first thought that popped into my head was, *where in the world am I going to get $10,000?* There will always be a faith test. God will always stretch you. He's like a physical trainer. He pushes you to the next level. Remember this, while you're going through the process, or learning His principals and meeting His prerequisites, He will always ask you to do something that's beyond your natural resources and capabilities. In fact, you're going to discover that most of what He tells you to do doesn't make sense—like Noah building an ark, or if you need wine for a wedding and He tells you to fill up six pots with water (John 2:1-7). The key to passing any test with God is found in verse 5: " Whatsoever He says to you, do it." If you could do it in your own power, or with your own resources, then you could take the credit for it. You might as well settle this right now: God gets all the glory. Here is my advice: whenever He requires you to step out in faith, do what Mary told those servants: "Whatever He says to you, do it."

My head gave me a lot of trouble. I knew I heard from God, however my mind kept trying to pull me back to the natural. How? Where? When? What? I had to fight myself. I had to make myself shut up. No wonder God told Joshua to put His Word first. As you put His Word in first place, it will settle your soul. As I walked out of the church that morning, I unconsciously reached into my pocket and noticed I had money in my pocket. It was thirteen dollars. I meant to put it on the altar while the pastor preached. I gave so much that morning that it slipped my mind. At the time, all of my checks had a comma in them. So when the Lord said to give my whole check, it wasn't minimum wage. He knew I enjoyed my job and the money I earned. It was my own money test. It was like the rich, young ruler, "one thing thou lackest" (Mark 10:21). I quickly turned around and found a deacon. I asked him to put it in the offering for me at the 10:00 a.m. service. When I left the church that morning, I had no money in my wallet, but I had taken up my cross and my life would never be the same (Genesis 22:12).

**Systematic Sowing**

On June 24, 2012, I sowed my first thousand dollar seed. Then, every week, I would sow a two hundred dollar seed on top of the tithe and general offering. I also gave love offerings and was a promise partner, which required a monthly seed. I sowed like I was out of my mind. As I sowed, I rose in status at the job, which meant more money. The more I made, the more I sowed. My mind screamed, but I sowed anyway. One day, while my reasoning yelled in my head, I blurted out, "Just do it!" My wife heard me and asked what I said. I answered, "Nothing, honey." It wasn't easy; it was a real battle. I sowed like clockwork. Every Wednesday and every Sunday. I sowed checks and cash systematically. Nothing interrupted my sowing. I turned the bills over to my wife and she had access to my account to pay the bills. I signed the checks. My focus was to sow and preach the Gospel.

At the New Year's church service that year, my bishop made a profound statement: "If you want to know where you'll be this time next year, it will be determined by the books you read." I went home and ordered two books, both by Dr. Leroy Thompson, Sr. *Money cometh to the body of Christ*, and *I'll never be broke another day in my life*. My life was about to take a monumental turn. This man knew something. I followed his teachings in books and online.

On May 19, 2013, I sowed a six hundred dollar seed and that made the ten thousand dollar pledge good. In that year, I gave $11,538.13. The next year, that increased to $14,404.14. On May

5, 2015, I was completely out of debt. Glory to God! I had sowed my way out.

One morning, while meditating in bed, the Lord spoke to me.

"Do you remember when I told you to give ten thousand dollars?"

I said, "Yes, Lord."

He then said, "What do you have in the bank now?"

I didn't know the answer. My wife handled the money and all the bills. I signed the checks. So I asked my wife how much I had in the account, and guess what? She said, "Ten thousand dollars."

I started out broke and in debt. After I went through some tests and met God's required prerequisites, I was debt-free with fragments left over (John 6:12).

**The Successful Seed Sower**

While going through that particular stage of my life, I picked up a few things. Some of them I received from the Holy Ghost, and others I picked up from my senior pastor. Also I had the honor of studying behind Apostle Leroy Thompson, Sr. and learning by percept and example. I would be remiss if I did not give you a few sowing principles. There is no true success without money. Don't be all deep and spiritual and stupid. You need money for your life, your family, and your assignment. In order to get to the successful place God wants you to be, you have to be a successful sower, period.

## Sow Some – Spend Some – Save Some

The God kind of success requires you to know how to operate in God's economy. You're going to have to be weaned off the world's system. God must become your source. Make sure you see your job for what it is: a source for seed.

Tithing and giving offerings helps you stay balanced. It keeps moving you forward; it keeps your priorities straight. It keeps you focused with your eyes on Him. Giving into the Kingdom is an act of honor. It shows your respect and reverence for God. When the magi went to see Him who was born king, they worshipped and they gave. Giving is worship. In the Old Testament, the people were taught not only how to worship, but how giving was an *act* of worship. In fact, they were commanded not to come before God empty-handed (Dueteronomy 16:16 NIV).

Here is my advice: whenever you have money, honor the Lord with your income. First, become a consistent tither. Second, become a systematic sower. Third, be a faithful steward. I operate under the principle of sow some, spend some, and save some.

A good steward understands that God owns everything. When God allows money to come into your hands, it must be dispersed properly. A good steward understands that, at some point, he must give an account of his stewardship. He also understands he must be faithful. The principle of "sow some, spend some, save some" will act as guardrails. They will keep you heading in the right direction so you won't go off the road.

"Sow some" is simple. Tithe and give offerings to your local church. There is no true success outside of the local church. You must be connected properly. I admonish you to study about the tithe. Know what you're doing. Don't be someone who drops an offering in a basket and has no clue what you did. When I tithe and give offerings, the first thing I do is read Malachi 3:10-12 and Proverbs 3:5-10. Then I write the check. Then I pray over it. By the time I put my offering in the basket at church, a spiritual transaction has already taken place. You don't go to the bank nonchalantly, do you? You know exactly what you're doing. You know how much you're depositing or withdrawing. Philippians 4:17 makes it clear the believer has an account in heaven. If you read the context in which that text speaks, you will find these believers were actively engaged in heaven's economy.

Most believers quote verses 13 and 19, but skip over everything before and in between. These believers were partners; they were involved with giving and receiving. Let me put this in natural terms: they made deposits and withdrawals. They weren't just church members; they were active members with the bank of heaven, and membership has its privileges. Glory to God! Hence, the apostle concludes by saying, "My God will supply all your needs."

This may sound strange to you, but I have natural and spiritual bank ledgers. The natural ones track my accounts on earth, while the spiritual ledgers track my giving, the tithe and offerings, as well as my giving to partners in the advancement of the Kingdom. If Jesus were to walk up to me today and say, "Give an account," I'd go in my bedroom and get the books from the last few years and say,

"Here you go." I record the tithe, my offerings, my seed, my giving to the poor, and love offerings. I take giving and receiving seriously. Successful people value money. They understand it's a currency; hence, it should flow. As you track your giving, you will notice year by year how you sow, flow, and grow. Once you connect properly, you will not only be an active participant in advancing the Kingdom of God, but you will simultaneously improve the quality of your life.

"Spend some" is also simple. Pay your bills. If you don't already have a system for responsible bill payment, mortgage, rent, insurance, or phone bills, then get one. Successful people know how to allocate funds. I am blessed to have a good wife. When we met, she already had a system in place. She never misses payments. She's systematic. I got in on her system like I got in on God's system. Don't forget to spend something on yourself, but everything in moderation.

Finally, "save some". As I already stated, don't be all spiritual and stupid. You should have a savings account. When you're able to create a portfolio, learn how to invest and get in the flow. Successful people are always expanding.

In conclusion, despite small beginnings, take your time and go through the process. Train yourself. Be a student of the Word. Prepare yourself so when God decides to spring a pop quiz on you, you're able to pass the test. Preparation, preparation, preparation. Success is not an accident. It doesn't drop on you like ripe cherries off a tree. It's a process of practicing principles and meeting prerequisites.

# Counseling – Command – Connection

You will never be truly successful until you are under command and receiving proper counseling. One of the hardest things for people to do is submit to someone else. From the time that we reached the age of accountability, we thought we knew it all. We think we know more than our parents, our teachers, and our elders. When the reality is no one knows everything except God. You and I only know what we've been taught. In fact, the main reason most of us are not as successful as we should be is because we've been taught wrong. You are the sum total of all that you've learned over the years. You are the product of whoever has taught, counseled, and instructed you. If you take a look at your life, you would see you are in the position you are in because of your associations and connections. Your personality, your values, and your perspective in life are all shaped by teaching, association, and environment.

When I joined the Army, one of the first things they did was strip me. They changed my clothes, my location, my thinking, and my name. I was no longer the civilian Geren Gatling; I was the soldier, Private Gatling. It felt like everything the military taught me was radical. I talked differently, walked differently, viewed life differently, and ate differently—everything was changed. Why did they do that? In retrospect, it's obvious: they wanted to turn me into what they called the "ultimate fighting man," the American infantryman. They knew I couldn't be all that I could be with my civilian mindset. My "have it your way" mentality would not get it done. I had to be to taught how to follow orders. It was imperative to understand the power of command.

Likewise, beloved, you will never be all that God wants you to be with an un-renewed mind. A person whose mind is not renewed with the Word of God will never submit to authority. When you don't understand the good, acceptable, and perfect will of God, you will question everything your leader says. "Why do I have to do that? That doesn't make any sense, why not do it this way? I'm anointed, too. I can do better than he can. I'm going to do it this way."

An uncommitted believer is in rebellion and will never eat the good of the land (Isaiah 1:19-20). I will never forget when I had to report to another man. He was a squad leader. I thought to myself, *Why do I need to talk to him? I need to talk to the platoon sergeant.* Every time I skipped that process, I got in trouble. They would never let me get away with it. I reported to the squad leader, the squad leader reported to the platoon sergeant, the platoon sergeant reported it to the lieutenant. The lieutenant reported to the captain and the captain reported to his superior. It was called the chain of command and if you broke it, there were always consequences.

God is not the author of confusion. He is a God of order and will not tolerate breaking the chain of command. He will place you in a church the same way the military places you at a base and will put people over you. Here are a few scriptures for you to mull over. Please stop and take the time to look them up; remember, we are talking about following instructions: Amos 3:6, 1 Peter 5:1-6, Hebrews 13:7,17. Now let us read this next verse together:

"Only be thou strong and very courageous, that thou mayest observe to do according to all the law, which Moses my servant commanded thee: turn not from it to the right hand or the left, that thou mayest prosper whithersoever thou goest" (Joshua 1:7, KJV).

The word "command" in one form or another is mentioned eight times in the first chapter of the book of Joshua. Please mark each one in your Bible.

Before God gave Joshua his marching orders, He reminded him of the power of command. Moses was the servant of the Lord, Joshua was the servant of Moses (Joshua 1:1). The officers of the people were under Joshua's command (Joshua 1:10). The people received their instructions from the leaders. The word "minister" in Joshua 1:1 is translated as "servant, assistant, or helper." God didn't allow Joshua to lead until he learned how to serve. He had to learn how to assist another person's ministry first. His connection to the successful ministry of Moses prepared him for his own success. It's extremely dangerous to skip the process. I know people (and so do you) who stepped out too quickly. They felt the call; they had an inward knowing that they were supposed to be doing something for God. They went out with no preparation, no training, no covering, and no pastoral blessing. If you haven't served, you have no biblical right to lead.

"Now after the death of Moses the servant of the Lord it came to pass that the Lord spoke unto Joshua the son of Nun saying, 'Moses my servant is dead, *now therefore arise, go*' " (Joshua 1:1-2a, emphasis mine).

Notice the timing and the sequence: "now, therefore, arise and go." It wasn't until after he assisted Moses and was trained—not before, but after the death of Moses. Beloved, there are some things that must die first. Your stubbornness must die. Your hidden agenda must die. Your un-submitted spirit must die. Please get this.

"You will never be truly successful until you are properly connected, and become a part of something or someone greater than yourself. If you want to be great you must learn how to serve" (Matthew 23:11-12).

Whatever God has called you to do, He will always connect you to someone who is already doing it. If you will submit to the training, then the mantle or the anointing and grace that's on the person you're connected to will be transferred to you. Anointings are transferred by connection and association.

"And Joshua the son of Nun was full of the spirit of wisdom; for Moses had laid his hands upon him. And the children of Israel heartened unto him, and did as the Lord commanded Moses" (Deuteronomy 34:9).

Notice how the people obeyed Joshua like they obeyed Moses. They obeyed Joshua because of his connection to the man of God. They knew he served under Moses. They saw him assist Moses in the wilderness. He had the training and the calling. He was an experienced leader. He had Moses' blessing because the man of God laid hands on him and there was transference. Success is transferable. It can be passed from one generation to another. Success is supposed to flow.

Your success in life is directly connected to who is counseling you.

"Blessed is the man who does not walk in the counsel of the wicked or stand in the way of sinners or sit in the seat of mockers" (Psalm 1:1).

When I came to Jesus, I had a myriad of issues. Turning my life over to Him was the best move I've ever made. After a series of wrong decisions got me in a mess, I finally made a good decision; success is a process of making good decisions.

When I left the back room of the church on October 17, 2010, I was on my way to heaven with my name in the Lamb's Book of Life. However, I had too much baggage for my trip. I had picked up a lot of bad habits while in the world. I was like a soldier who had come home from war. I've seen some things and experienced things that had a traumatic effect on me. I needed some professional help. Homelessness drove me crazy. Drugs drove me crazy. Years in prison had an effect on the mind that drove me nuts. Recidivism is so high because most people released from prison didn't get the proper help while incarcerated, nor do they get proper counseling when they are released.

I've been to at least seven drug programs, relapsed seven times, went back to jail at least seven times, and had probation officer after probation officer. Why didn't anything work for me? As I sat in the pew one Sunday morning, I knew I was in trouble. Here I was: saved, but damaged. I remember I was always scared. I still had numerous criminal charges to face. I had bad credit, bad health, bad family relations, bad thinking—I was still jacked up. Saved, but still suffering inside. The people around me didn't know, but I'm so glad the great Counselor knew! He knew exactly how to fix me. One songwriter said, "He didn't bring us this far to leave us, he didn't teach us to swim to let us drown. He didn't build his home in us to move away, he didn't lift us up to let us down" (The Imperials).

He had a plan for me. He didn't take me off the street to abandon me. I remember sitting in the pew terrified and not knowing how I was going to get out of the mess I was in. But right in the midst of all the shouting and preaching I heard the Lord say, "I have called him to be like Moses, I am going to use him to bring you out." He was speaking about my senior pastor Bishop Staples. After the Lord told me that, I intuitively knew I had to get closer. I moved up to the second row and listened with the intent to do what Bishop Staples said. We have a rather large church, so I knew the chances of spending quality time with him were slim.

It was in that pew that I learned an invaluable lesson. It felt like every time I had a question or needed direction or correction, the pastor said something that addressed my concern. It was spooky. I never told him what I thought or struggled with, yet it felt like he could read my mind. A lot of times, I thought somebody told him and spied on me! I was still going through withdrawals from cocaine and was extremely paranoid. The strange thing about it was, as he would minister the Word of God, I started changing. I found out that I didn't need to sit behind his desk and be counseled; the Holy Spirit counseled me from the pulpit to the pew. As I put that counseling into practice, I began to notice a big change. My relatives saw me changing; people knew something had happened to me. Every time someone asked me about it, I always said the same thing: "I started going to this church." Please listen to me clearly: Jesus works through the local church. If you're not properly connected to a local church, you will never be truly successful. Proper connection is defined by your attending worship, tithing to the church, and submitting to the pastor. You must be connected and committed to your God-appointed leader.

**You Are Not Connected**

Has this ever happened to you: you settle down in some restaurant or establishment, take out you electronic device and it won't work function correctly. You fumble around and then go to your settings and these words pop up: "You are not connected," and you get an ah-ha moment. The first time that happened, I laughed at myself. Once I joined a network and put in the password it said, "connected," and lo and behold, the device would work. I have discovered when my life is out of balance, I need to check my connection. It doesn't matter how talented you are. It doesn't matter how good you look or how educated you are. If you're not connected properly, you are like an electronic device that has capability, but no power.

I am convinced one of our biggest problems is we don't know who we are or how we were designed to function. You were not designed to function independently from God. When an automobile company designs an automobile, they provide you with a manual. The manual helps you to get your vehicle to operate at an optimum level. It tells you what kind of gas, how much air, when to change the oil, and so forth. If you violate those simple instructions, you invariably end up broken down on the side of the road. Simple mechanical problems could have been prevented by following the manual.

I've found my life on the side of road numerous times until I began to follow God's manual. Once I found out who I was and how I was designed to operate, my ride through life went from stop-and-go to flowing through the traffic of life. First of all, you are a spiritual being created in the image and likeness of God. You can find that in the first page of God's manual in Genesis 1:26: "And God said, 'Let us make man in our image, after our likeness: and let them have dominion over the fish of the sea, and over the fowl of the air and over the cattle, and over all the earth, and over every creeping thing that creeps upon the earth.' ". So if

I'm created in His image and likeness, I now need to know what is God's image? What is God's likeness? From our youth, we've been programmed to identify ourselves based on race, pedigree, environment, the color of our skin, and other "isms." The reality is, the Manufacturer of Heaven made us all of one blood (Acts 17:26-28). We are God's offspring. If I walked up to you and said, "Identify yourself," what would be your reply? Would you begin to tell me about your roots in another country? Or how many degrees you have, or talk about your gender, your accomplishments or some other natural reasoning?

Note this: *if you want to maximize your effectiveness, and be all that God has predestined you to be, you must know who you truly are.* When you don't know who you truly are, you will begin to measure yourself by others, categorize yourself in a particular group, and identify yourself by media catch phrases like, "this life matters," or "that life matters," when the truth is, all lives matter. You don't find your identity by looking without; you find it by looking within.

Let's briefly examine God's manual on the subtopic, *according to God's manual, who am I?* In order to know who I am, I have to first know who God is, because according to Genesis 1:26, I am created in His image and likeness. Let's begin by examining what Jesus said about God. In the gospel of John 4:24, Jesus makes this definitive statement: "God is a Spirit." Now why should we accept Jesus' testimony? I'm glad you asked. Let's check the manual for that answer. John 1:1-2 says, "In the beginning was the Word, and the Word was with God and the Word was God." The same was in the beginning with God (John 1:14) and the Word was made flesh. There is a lot of information in those few verses, but let's keep it simple. Allow me to paraphrase: Jesus was there in the beginning with God, so if anybody ought to know what God is like, it would have to be Jesus, isn't that right? I mean, whom else are you going to ask? Do you remember when Jesus healed a blind man in John chapter 9? (Please take a moment and read verses 1-22.)

This man was born blind, but when he was brought before the Pharisees for questioning they didn't want to accept his testimony that he was born that way (verse 18). That is, until they asked his parents. Let me ask you a rhetorical question: why didn't they ask you? Let me state the obvious: they asked the parents because the parents were there in the beginning when the child was born, and if anybody ought to know about the child, it had to be the parents. So I say again: Jesus was there in the beginning with God, and if anybody knows what God is like, it would have to be Jesus, because in the beginning was the Word (Jesus) and the Word (Jesus) was with God.

Jesus, the one who was there in the beginning said, "God is a Spirit." Now, since God is a Spirit, and I am created in His image and likeness, then I must be a spirit, right? I mean, when your cat has a litter, are you shocked the kittens look like the momma? How about when your dog has puppies, are you surprised they look like the momma? So why is it so shocking that, as God's offspring, you're made after the similitude of God (James 3:9)? Did you take a moment to read that verse? The word "similitude" in the Greek means "likeness". Based upon God's manual, I have a right to declare, *"I am first and foremost a spirit being created in the image and likeness of God."*

If you want to know your natural roots, you can visit ancestry.com. If you want to know your spiritual roots, read Genesis 1:26. You are a spirit. Let's go a step further. Back to the manual: "For there are three that bear record in heaven, the Father the Word, and the Holy Ghost: and these three are one" (1 John 5:7). Again, there is a lot in that verse, but let's keep it simple. That verse plainly says the Father, the Word (Jesus), and the Holy Ghost are one. Let's say it another way: they are in perfect harmony. They are in perfect agreement. If I'm created in His likeness, then there must be a scripture in God's manual that supports that fact. .

"And the very God of peace sanctify you wholly, and I pray your whole spirit and soul and body be preserved blameless unto the coming of our Lord Jesus Christ" (1 Thessalonians 5:23).

Notice this verse clearly states I am a spirit, I have a soul, and live in a body. I'm a triune being. In other words, the same way that the Godhead is comprised of the Father, the Son, and Holy Ghost, I am comprised of spirit, soul, and body.

It would do you well to do a study on the Godhead (also known as the Trinity). Among other things, you will find the Hebrew word for God is *elohim*. It's a uni-plural word. The prefix "uni" means one. "Plural" simply means more than one. It's sort of like the word "people;" we know it means one group, but we also know there is more than one person in the group. The word "God" is the same way. We know from scripture that the Lord our God is one Lord (Deuteronomy 6:4), but we also know there is more than one person in the Godhead, and that is the Father, the Son, and the Holy Ghost. When you look in the mirror, how many people do you see? Of course you only see one. However, according to God's manual in 1 Thessalonians 5:23, we know as a being that is created in the image and likeness of God, you are comprised of spirit, soul, and body. In order to flow in the kind of success that God has designed for you, it is imperative you identify yourself as a spirit being created in the image and likeness of God. You have a soul and you live in a physical body. It is also important to get your total being to agree as one. When you made Jesus the Lord of your life, you were reconnected to the life source. Like a cell phone that was drained of power and then reconnected to a charger, it takes time to be recharged. You literally have to leave it alone for a time and let the phone go through the process. If you decide to unplug it after five minutes, it won't be long before you are in the same position you were a moment ago: powerless. Beloved, never underestimate the power of connection. You have to plug in to God. You were designed to connect to Him. Our Father, the God of success, is so awesome. When we reconnected to Him by faith in the blood of Jesus, He put us in a place to recharge.

"The righteous shall flourish like a palm tree: he shall grow like a cedar of Lebanon. Those that be planted in the house of the Lord shall flourish in the courts of our God. They shall still bring forth fruit in old age; they shall be fat and flourishing" (Psalm 92:12-14).

*Never underestimate the power of being connected to a local church*

Why does God place us in a church when we get saved? Why is it so important to be planted in the house of the Lord? What does my success in life have to do with my connection to a local church? I will use my own experience to answer those questions. When I left the church building that Sunday morning after receiving Jesus as Lord, it would be three days before I would return for midweek Bible study. Folks, life drained me. The vicissitudes of life suck the energy out of you. Sunday morning services charged me like a battery and life would draw it out. If I missed Bible study, I found I would be powerless. I didn't have the strength to resist the temptations of everyday life. Remember: I was saved, but I still had twenty-seven criminal charges against me. I was still homeless. I was still broke. I still had no family connections. All I knew was the street. The church was my restoration center. It was my filling station. It was my hospital. It was my rehabilitation center. I was like a car that was in a bad accident. Even if you put gas in me, I could go down the road, but I was still damaged. When I went to church, every service would work on a different problem. Every sermon took a dent out. Every worship service tuned me up. Every Bible study was like an oil change. I finally caught on; my going to church was like a car regularly stopping at the gas station. It was a necessary connection.

I was in line one day waiting for my turn to vote. I was in a local school. I happened to look up and saw a sign above the door that said, "multipurpose room." In my spirit, I heard the Lord say, "The local church is like that," and I knew exactly what He meant. That auditorium is for meetings, events, PTA, emergency drills, school activities, and even a voting location among other things. People are there for different reasons, much like the church. The local church is like a hospital to heal people. It's like a gym to keep people spiritually fit. It's like a buffet where people go to get spiritual food. The church is a wellness center. Your level of success in life is directly connected to your well being. Your well being is directly connected to your association with your local church. Never underestimate the power of being connected to a local church.

***Flourish: to bloom, to grow; to blossom to be successful or to thrive***

Notice where Psalm 92:12-14 says, "the righteous flourish," we bloom in the house of God. The local church is enriched with spiritual soil. It has nutrients in it that cannot be found anywhere else. If we will sit still long enough, the components in the church that are necessary for Christian growth will take hold and cause us to be successful. That is why it's ridiculous for a believer to church hop. How do you expect a flower to grow if you keep plucking it up? If God plants you in a particular place, don't you think He knows what He's doing?

"The Lord God planted a garden eastward in Eden; and there He put the man whom He had formed" (Genesis 2:8).

Do you think God knew what He was doing when He planted a garden in Eden? Do you think He knew what He was doing when He put the man in the garden? He put the man in a place where he could thrive. He put him in a place where he could exercise his God-given abilities. Everything he needed was in the garden. Beloved, everything you need to blossom is in your local church. Your pastor is like a gardener; he tends to you. He waters you with the Word of God. He skillfully cuts away dead leaves and fertilizes you. He wants you to be beautiful and enriched so you can be a delightful sight for the world to see. You have to trust the pastor (gardener) that God put over you. You were planted with the intent to flourish. You are designed to be prosperous. Your spiritual DNA will do what it was designed to do if you would settle in the ground that you were planted in. Stay connected, stay planted, and abide in the soil of success. Eventually, the success of your pastor and that established ministry will flow into you. Whatever is in the soil will inevitably get into the plant. When a believer disconnects from his or her parent church and joins another church, then decides to disconnect from that church and joins another church or goes back to the parent church, that person becomes a hybrid. Instead of being what God intended you to be, you become some kind of mixed nut. Have you seen people like that? God intended them to be spiritual mustangs, but because they cross-bred in another church, they turned out to be spiritual donkeys!. Flourish in the soil in which you were planted. Stay connected.

**Perfect Well Being**

> The elder unto the well beloved Gaius, whom I love in the truth. Beloved, I wish above all things that thou mayest prosper and be in health, even as thy soul prospereth. For I rejoiced greatly, when the brethren came and testified of the truth that is in thee, even as thou walkest in the truth. I have no greater joy than to hear that my children walk in the truth. (3 John 1:1-4)

I'm going to have to get my soul well if I'm going to be truly successful.

It is the Father's earnest desire that we prosper in every facet of life. When you think about it, isn't that what every parent wants? Don't you want your children to excel in life? Well if you, being natural, want the best for your children, how much more does your Father in heaven want for His children to thrive in their lives? Any parent does his or her best to provide for the child and secure a bright future. However, there comes a point where the child grows up and is required to do something. Success doesn't fall on you like ripe cherries from a tree. Desire must be coupled with action. Dreams must grow a pair of legs. Notice in the above text that God's desire for you to prosper and be in health is directly related to the condition of your soul. The Amplified Bible gives us more clarity: "Beloved, I pray that in every way you may succeed and prosper and be in good health physically, just as I know your soul prospers spiritually" (3 John 1:2).

Notice the phrase, "just as." Let me say it another way: "I want the rest of your life to prosper just like your soul." Everything must be in balance. You have to be successful on the inside before you can be successful on the outside. This man, Gauis, to whom the letter was addressed, had a secret to success that worked in three places.

Let's look again at 3 John 1:1-4:

> The elder unto the well-beloved Gaius whom I love *in the truth* Beloved I wish above all things that thou mayest prosper, and be in health even as thy soul prosperth. For I rejoiced greatly when the brethren came and testified of *truth that is in thee* even as thou *walkest in the truth* I have no greater joy than to hear that my children *walkest in the truth*.

I emphasized the three-step process with italics. He was first and foremost *in the truth*. Second, the *truth was in him,* and third, he *walked in the truth*. Can you see that? His success wasn't automatic. If you read the entire letter, you will see the Apostle John said he heard about his success. He said the "brothers came and bore witness of your success." He didn't say "brother," singular. He said "brothers" plural, meaning several people have said you have it going on. You're not only helping church folk, but strangers. Anybody who knows anything about life knows good and well you can't help people like you want to without money and or spiritual insight into life. Gaius' success began to overflow to the point it had an effect on the locals and was even heard of from abroad. It didn't just happen; he *made* it happen. He got in the truth, he got the truth in him, and then he walked it out. My beloved, if you want God's kind of success to flow in your life and then into your local community and abroad, then you also must get the truth to flow from the inside out. The Apostle John revealed to us three fundamental principles that worked for Gaius and will work for you. Let's examine them more closely:

Pilate therefore said unto him, "Art thou a king then?" Jesus answered, "Thou sayest that I am a king. To this end was I born, and for this cause came I into the world, that I should bear witness unto the truth. Every one that is of the truth heareth my voice." Pilate saith unto him, "What is truth?" (John 18:37-38)

Pilate asked a good question. What is truth? Successful people normally do ask for clarity. The Apostle John walked with Jesus. He mentions things in his gospel that the other gospel writers did not.

"And you shall know the truth, and the (Truth) shall make you free" (John 8:32).

"Jesus said unto him, 'I am the way, the (Truth) and the life: no man comes unto the Father but by me' " (John 14:6).

"Sanctify them through thy *Truth*, thy word is *Truth*" (John 17:17).

In my ministry, I often share with people that there is no answer like a Bible answer. When you want clarity on a subject, always go back to the Word. This doesn't mean you neglect other sources of information. Successful people know how to keep things down the middle of the road. The key is to measure everything by the Word. So, let's answer Pilate's question in light of the word of God. What is truth? According to God's manual, Jesus is the truth and the Word is the truth. Do you remember what we discussed in the last chapter from John's gospel in chapter one? "In the beginning was the Word, and the Word was with God and the Word was God. And the Word was made flesh and dwelt among us" (John 1:1,14). When we rightly divide the Word of God (2 Timothy 2:15), it is clear Jesus and the Word of God are one.

Let's apply the law of parallel truth to what this same apostle said about the success of Gaius. Allow me to paraphrase into order to bring clarity: "The elder unto the well-beloved Gauis, whom I love in the truth (I love in the Word; I love in Jesus). Beloved, I earnestly desire you to prosper financially, and I hope that prosperity will flow into your body and keep you healthy, the same way you are prospering on the inside. It gave me great joy when several people came and spoke of your success in every facet of your life. They spoke of the truth that is in you (of the Word that is in you, of the Jesus in you), even as you walk in the truth; even as you walk in the Word, even as you walk in Jesus). Nothing thrills me like hearing my children have received a revelation and walk in the truth. Walking in the Word means walking in Jesus."

That's the Geren Gatling translation. The fundamental key to God's kind of success is to get in Jesus, then get in His Word, and lastly walk that Word out. In other words, the Word of God must permeate our entire lifestyles. Jesus put it best in John's gospel: "If ye abide in me, and my words abide in you, ye shall ask what ye will, and it shall be done unto you" (John 15:7).

In order to prosper no matter where you go or what you do, there must be a proper word flow. The Word of God must be exalted above all you do. I never leave my house without a word from God. I kneel down beside the bed with my Bible and call upon the name of the Lord. I often say:

> Lord, you have exalted your word above all your name (Psalm 138:2) and I too exalt your word above all my name, above my status, above my degree, above my title, and above my street knowledge. You have forever settled your word in heaven (Psalm 119:89) and I settle it here on earth. Your word will feed my spirit, for your words are spirit and they are life (John 6:63). I live by every word that proceeds from your mouth. My inner man is renewed by your word day by day (2 Corinthians 4:16). Your word restores my soul and renews my mind (Romans 12:2). Your word renews my strength, quickens me, and makes me

alive (Psalm 119:107). Your word is my medicine according to Proverbs 4:20-22. I give your word my attention; I incline my ear to your sayings. I will not let them depart from my eyes, I will keep them in the midst of my heart; they are life to me and medicine to my whole being. I thank you for your holy apostles, prophets, evangelist, pastors, and teachers who feed me your word in order to bring me to maturity, and equip me for ministry so I can edify the body of Christ (Ephesians 4:11-13). Thank you for your grace to be a doer of your word and not a hearer only. Thank you for my primary overseer, Bishop Glen A. Staples, who feeds me the Word of God and watches over my soul (1 Peter 5:2, Hebrews 13:7,17). Thank you for my instructor, Apostle Leroy Thompson Sr., who teaches me about heaven's econonmy and how to flow in Kingdom finance. Thank you for Kenneth Copeland and Kenneth Hagin who teach me about faith and healing (1 Corinthians 4:15). Thank you for the Holy Spirit, whom you have sent to be my teacher and my guide. Holy Spirit, I thank you for unveiling the truth to my spirit, bringing the word back to my remembrance, and showing me things to come (John 14:26, John 16:13). I humble myself before the authority of your Word and declare I have eyes to see and perceive, ears to hear and understand (Matthew 13:16). As always, my goal is to increase in the fruits of righteousness, walk in divine health, and walk in divine wealth to the glory of God the advancement of your Kingdom in Jesus' name, amen.

Then I get off my knees and give the Word of God my attention. I study my lessons daily that I teach and preach on the air, as well as listen to my instructors on the internet on the subjects of faith, healing, and finance. I understand my success is directly connected to my willingness and obedience to God's Word (Isaiah 1:19). I understand if I want the success of Gaius, the success of Joshua, and the success of the man in Psalm 1, I have to do want they did. All of them put the Word first. Joshua put it in his mouth; he mediated, and put it into action (Joshua 1:8). The man in Psalm 1 delighted himself in the Word and mediated upon it until he flourished like a tree planted by the rivers of living water (Psalm 1:3). Gaius made up his mind to live in the truth; he got it in him until it affected everything about him. I call it perfect well being. I stumbled onto that phrase while studying one day.

2 Peter 1:2 (AMP): "Grace and peace (that special sense of spiritual well-being) be multiplied to you in the true, intimate knowledge of God and of Jesus."

My curiosity led me to ask the question: what is spiritual well being? The writer translated the word "peace." So I dug a little deeper and looked up the word "peace" for myself. As I mentioned before, the Bible is an Eastern book translated from Hebrew and Greek. Peter was a Jewish man. When Jewish people say "peace" they don't put up two fingers trying to be hip, or cool, like modern Western society.

According to *Strong's Concordance* 7965, the word "peace" or *shalom* means "completeness, wholeness, health, peace, welfare, safety soundness, tranquility, prosperity, perfectness, fullness, rest, harmony, the absence of agitation or discord." *Shalom* comes from the root verb *shalom,* meaning, "to be complete, perfect and full." In Modern Hebrew, the obviously related word *shelem* means, "to pay for," and *shulam* means, "to be fully paid."

That doesn't leave anything out, does it? Glory to God! It is important to remember Jesus paid it all. Notice that last clause of the above paragraph: *to be fully paid.* Jesus is concerned about your well being. In John 10:10, He called it "an abundant life." A life that flows from your innermost being through your soul, into your body, your finances, your relationships and everything within your sphere of influence, and consummates when you get to heaven.

I love calling it "perfect well being." It means coming to a place where nothing is missing, nothing is broken, all your needs met, and you're out of debt. It is where you have a vibrant relationship with God, and that relationship affects everything around you and about you. A sound mind, good health, and abundant supplies. It's the good life, the life that Jesus intended for you to have, and died for you to have—a life that overflows. This is not an ordinary life. It's beyond normal; it's supernatural. The seed of success that God planted in you at the new birth is supposed to cause you to grow and flow naturally into the supernatural. Say this out loud: *I'm supposed to be successful. An apple doesn't try and struggle to develop into an apple; it stays connected to the tree and does what it's designed to do. I don't need to struggle; I'll stay connected to Jesus and His Word and will naturally do what I was designed to do. I'm wired to win; it's in my spiritual DNA. A dog is supposed to bark, a cat should meow, a bird should fly and I'm supposed to rule and dominate in life like my Daddy in heaven!*

Remember this my friend: it's impossible to be truly successful until you realize you're *supposed* to be successful. Success is supposed to flow. It has never been and never will be all about you.

# Let the rivers flow

I don't want to leave the impression that I have all the answers, or even worse, that I have it all together, because I can assure you that I have not arrived. Like the Apostle Paul I press towards the mark for the prize (Phillipians 3:12-14). I do, however, want to leave a mark in your heart that cannot be erased. I want to share this fountain of living water that I have found. In my quest for success I have met plenty of people who thirst for more. They desire more, they are looking for more. People are trying all kinds of things in order to find fulfillment.

My past life was dry and painful. I suffered trying to do things my way. I slept on the floors of drug houses, jailhouses, courthouses, and park benches miserable and worn down. Failure flowed into every part of my life. I was drowning in failure, floating on a log of defeat in the midst of the sea of life, stranded and far from the peaceful shore. Nothing worked for me until I turned to Jesus. He was the missing link. Life had no meaning until I encountered Him.

He is the God of success. Who is more successful than God? When He comes into your heart, that success is supposed to have a positive affect on your life. That success is supposed to flow. Eternal life is more than just going to heaven; it's the life of God himself taking up residence in you. He wants to live in you and walk in you and make His home in you. He wants to guide you through the vicissitudes of life. He never intended for you to live life independently of Him. From the very beginning He wanted you to be successful. Once you accept Him into your life, you have to learn to walk with Him. There is a life-long process of yielding to him so that He can order your steps. The fact of the matter is He has a plan for your life. He wants to reveal that plan to you and bring it to fruition in your life. We have only a glimpse of where we are going, but the Father has a full view of our destinies. We have to let him take us by the hand and walk us through it. It's a walk of faith. Like a child who leaves the house with his natural father who says we're going to Disneyland, the child has an image of what it's going to be like, but no clue of all that the trip entails. Yet he believes and takes Poppy by the hand. We learn to flow with God; we learn to trust Him and lean on Him daily. We eventually come to a place where we can receive the revelation that we can't live without Him. He becomes a necessity. Like water, this is not a one cup experience. I have to drink of Him daily. Life is dry without Him. The average adult human body is up to sixty-five percent water. About seventy percent of the earth's surface is covered by water, from the oceans to the vapor in the air and the very soil you walk on. Neither this earth nor we would exist without it. There is a parallel truth there. In God we live and move and have our being. He's in us, all around us; by Him all things consist. We would not exist without him! When we receive Jesus into our hearts, a well of water was opened within us (John 4:14). That well was intended to spring up and flow. It starts by being well with our soul; then it flows into every part of our lives. We learn to draw from that well daily. We learn to allow it to refresh our minds and bodies.

God is concerned about our welfare. He wants to have an active part in every area of our lives. He wants us to be successful. Our lives should be so full of success that it overflows into the lives of the people around us. The well of water within us should become a river that flows to the masses. I have discovered that within me is a life force that was designed to put me over in life. It is important to let the river flow. Allow God to flow through you. Yield to Him so that He can use you as His channel of mercy—an extension of His grace. He wants to reach the people around you, and you are that vehicle he's going to use.

As we learn to flow with Him, we learn not to block or clog up that flow with unbelief and unforgiveness. We eventually come to the revelation that all things are relative, and we're all connected. Like the pipes in a house are connected on purpose and for a purpose, the pipes in the basement aren't jealous of the pipes in the kitchen. The pipes in the bathroom are bickering with the pipes in the master bedroom. When the toilet is stopped up, it affects the whole house. When the sink in the kitchen is clogged it disrupts the household. Those pipes were designed to be free of debris so that they can let the water flow. I'm connected to you, you're connected to me, and we are all connected to God. The God of success wants to flow from heart to heart, from person to person and from nation to nation. When we envy one another and fight and divide into groups, it clogs the flow. The reality is we need each other to survive. Lakes and rivers, oceans and clouds work together. One flows into the other in perfect harmony. Even the animal kingdom teaches us to flow together. The fish have a way of existing together. The birds soar together, and the cattle walk together. We too should walk together—black and white, male and female. The enemy has found a way to divide us. What makes the medical doctor any better than the mechanic? What makes a politician better than the public school teacher? The fireman needs the police officer. The dentist needs the mechanic. You're successful in your field for others, not yourself. Your success is supposed to flow to your fellow man. Please get this. We need each other. Let the love flow. Let the blood of Jesus flow. Let faith flow. Let the rivers flow. Let success flow.

The book you are reading was never about me. The time and money invested in this book was all about you. It was my intent from the very beginning to be a blessing to you. I wasn't thinking about money or fame, I was thinking about you. All I could see was someone in a seemingly impossible situation, and I wanted to be the person who says "It's not over, you can come out. This situation can turn around." My life was on the brink of death in every facet of life: spiritually, emotionally, physically, financially and socially. When I found Jesus, I found success. If you gave your life to Jesus as a result of reading this book, then my success flowed to you. Your job now is to allow the success in you to flow into every facet of your life and then to those around you. Success is not selfish. Take the principles in this book and put them into practice. Find out your purpose in life and pursue it with the intent of having a positive lasting influence on humanity. When I leave this earth, my success will remain. Every video, every message, every book sold, will remain to help those coming behind me. My success will flow. I challenge you to do the same. Let the success flow.

www.ingramcontent.com/pod-product-compliance
Ingram Content Group UK Ltd.
Pitfield, Milton Keynes, MK11 3LW, UK
UKHW022216230426